Too Many Midnights

With Honesty, Sensitivity and Gentle Beauty, Rod McKuen Brings to Us Once Again His Unlimited Gifts of Loving and Sharing . . .

"That Rod McKuen has become the bestselling poet in America is a splendid thing, because simply he is one of the best lyrical poets in America— and it is a joy when hundreds of thousands, not just a few, recognize a major poet when they read or hear one." —*Los Angeles Herald Examiner*

". . . he composes poetry as hymns to love."
—New York *Daily News*

". . . he is capable of rendering awareness into perceptions of small but haunting truths."
—*Los Angeles Times*

A Biplane Book

Rod McKuen
Too Many Midnights

PUBLISHED BY POCKET BOOKS NEW YORK

A Biplane Book

Another *Original* publication of POCKET BOOKS

 POCKET BOOKS, a Simon & Schuster division of
GULF & WESTERN CORPORATION
1230 Avenue of the Americas, New York, N.Y. 10020

Copyright © 1981 by Rod McKuen

Cover and back cover photographs by Edward Habib McKuen

Photographs by Hy Fujita, Alan Catt, David Hume Kennerly, Edward
Habib McKuen, Rod McKuen, Wayne Massie, David Nutter, Ed
Thrasher, Ralph Crane.

DESIGN: JACQUES CHAZAUD

ISBN: 0-671-43111-0

First Pocket Books printing June, 1981

10 9 8 7 6 5 4 3 2 1

POCKET and colophon are trademarks of Simon & Schuster.

Printed in the U.S.A.

BY ROD McKUEN

BOOKS

Prose
    Finding My Father
    An Outstretched Hand
    A Book of Days

Poetry
    And Autumn Came
    Stanyan Street & Other Sorrows
    Listen to the Warm
    Lonesome Cities
    In Someone's Shadow
    Caught in the Quiet
    Fields of Wonder
    And to Each Season
    Come to Me in Silence
    Moment to Moment
    Celebrations of the Heart
    Beyond the Boardwalk
    The Sea Around Me
    Coming Close to the Earth
    We Touch the Sky
    The Power Bright and Shining
    The Beautiful Strangers (Fall 1981)

Collected Poems
    Twelve Years of Christmas
    A Man Alone
    With Love . . .
    The Carols of Christmas
    Seasons in the Sun
    Alone
    *The Rod McKuen Omnibus
    Hand in Hand
    Love's Been Good to Me
    Looking for a Friend
    Too Many Midnights

Music Collections
    The McKuen/Sinatra Songbook
    New Ballads
    At Carnegie Hall
    McKuen/Brel: Collaboration
    28 Greatest Hits
    Jean and Other Nice Things
    McKuen Country
    Through European Windows
    Greatest Hits, Vol. I
    Greatest Hits, Vol. II   *Available only in Great Britain

MAJOR FILM SCORES

The Prime of Miss Jean Brodie
A Boy Named Charlie Brown
Joanna
The Unknown War
Disney's Scandalous John
The Borrowers
Lisa Bright and Dark
Emily
Steinbeck's Travels with Charley

CLASSICAL MUSIC

Ballet
Americana, R.F.D.
Point/Counterpoint
Seven Elizabethan Dances
The Minotaur (Man to Himself)
Volga Song
Full Circle
The Plains of My Country
Dance Your Ass Off
The Man Who Tracked the Stars

Opera
The Black Eagle

Concertos
For Piano & Orchestra
For Cello & Orchestra
For Orchestra & Voice
For Guitar & Orchestra
#2 for Piano & Orchestra
For Four Harpsichords
Seascapes for Piano

Symphonies, Symphonic Suites, etc.
Symphony No. 1
Symphony No. 2
Ballad of Distances
The City
Symphony No. 3
Symphony No. 4
4 Quartets for Piano & Strings
4 Trios for Piano & Strings
Adagio for Harp & Strings
Rigadoon for Orchestra

This book
is for
Singo and Ingrid.

Author's Note

This book comes after a long year of work. Work that has taken me to several countries—including two trips from America to Australia.

After many stops and starts, I had finally finished *Too Many Midnights* more than thirteen months ago . . . yet seeing the finished manuscript when I returned to New York in January of 1981, I decided that I felt differently about what I had originally written.

On re-reading the work, the final version seemed very "down" to me. I'm not sure why. But I decided to start again. Whether any writer feels completely good about something he commits to paper . . . a collection of work already published or the newest child emerging from his typewriter (in this case, both circumstances apply) is doubtful. But this is a better book than the first—as the next anthology will be better still, and I can live with this collection with a certain unexplainable ease.

Too Many Midnights takes love apart—but unlike some things I have done, it puts it back together again. I'm pleased with that. I like the way the new title poem works, and "Whistle Stops Revisited" pleases me enough to want to include yet another version of it in a book I'm working on for Simon & Schuster entitled *The Beautiful Strangers*.

The poem about Edna St. Vincent Millay was written with love and dedicated to my editor, Margaret Blackstone.

I have included for the first time in a paperback anthology two poems that readers have long requested, "Now I Have the Time" and part of "Stanyan Street." Still it seems to me that this anthology includes more new work than any of the five books previously published by Pocket Books.

Rod McKuen
March 1981

Contents

Too Many Midnights

What each of us is looking for
lies not within the midnight
                    or the stars
and not within ourselves.

TOO MANY MIDNIGHTS

Alone, I've watched the midnights go
two, three, five, sometimes ten or more
in a ragged, rusty, ugly row.

Ragged because without a sharing
midnight has no special form.
The clock will tick it off
as only one more minute
in yet another uneventful hour.

Rusty, because not even golden moons
appear as gold when seen through spyglasses
or the single naked eye.

Ugly, because one man's thoughts on beauty
make no sense unless explained aloud,
half aloud or with no words at all
                        to some one else.

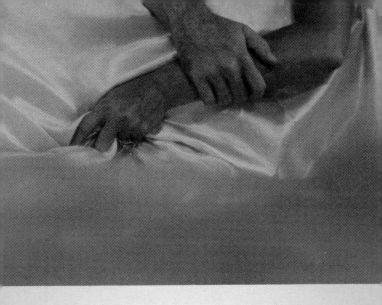

It is my belief that in my life
there are too many midnights
and yet not stars enough
within the midnight sky
to wish upon.
But I have never been
a man who followed his beliefs
to self-distortion
or disrupted them enough
that left behind,
they become unrecognizable.

So I have not deserted
that night sky yet
though deep inside me
is an ache, a bend however slight
that pleads and even orders me
to cast my eyes toward the ground
away from yet another hopeless hope.

An ache
is just an ache
and nothing more
and I will not be
ordered to give in by pain
or even lack of progress.
I defy a headache
or a stomach grumble
to order me away from hope.

The most that I am willing
              to bargain over
is a halving of the midnights
exploring some, ignoring others.

Even then the risk is great.
Suppose I miss a certain helping star,
one willing to be runner for me
explainer of my dark desire
to that one who knots my tongue
when I, myself, try putting words
                    that work together?

The chance for that to happen
is a chance I cannot, will not
abrogate to pain's decision.

Though pain pulls me,
it is but one end
of this tangled tug-of-war.
Night insists as much
and as the midnights pass
and show no sign of slowing
I'll reach out and catch one
by the neck or tail
once I'm sure someone is here
to savor and to share it with me.

I am not sad,
sorry for myself,
nor do I feel cheated.

But you and all the stars
as you go traveling
will not meet another man
              more impatient
or closer to the starting gate.

MIND MINDER

A butterfly flies up
inside my head,
consuming all my early years
the memory of just yesterday,
other loves and lives
I might have known or knew.

He sits and eats away
within that place I've lived
where he now lives.

Please remember for me
all those things
that need remembering.
Let me use your head
            as mine.

I ask that you
attempt to lead me,
to carry me aloft
bend down to scoop me up,
to ferry me across my life
as you would a child
across a too deep river.
You are the end of me,
and my new beginning.

You are my brother
            and my wife.
My lover and my son.
My mother and my husband
                my teacher
and the one I long to teach.

The woman
that I dreamed of finding
the friend who never was.

You transcend gender,
eliminate September,
add another month of Sundays
to a calendar well worn.

I will be for you
           whatever works.
I will work to make you *be*,
while you eliminate
the buzzing, ringing sound
that permeates my brain
           of late.

A butterfly
and maybe more
is buzzing in my head.
If he should eat it all away
you've head enough for both of us.

If caterpillars crawl
down through my brain
you've brain enough
so I'll not worry
over trivialities.

OCTOBER

The crushing fear we seldom speak of
is no less real
because it's only thought about.

It is the sorrow given credence
when we see the child
held up to ridicule and then abuse.

Adults that act not like adults,
or even children in their games,
but those parading down the street
or in the L and box-shaped room
in the guise of all the monsters
and the demons in our younger years
we thought we'd finally exorcised.

The fear we seldom speak about
is the loss of gentleness
that traps us when we least expect it
or let our guard down even for a minute.

So in the night and through the day
our eyes must only stay half-closed,
lest gentleness be carried off
by monsters far too evil to have names.

A TOAST

Amid the toasts
and glasses raised
on holidays and special nights
let none of us forget
            each other
that in the scheme of things
with mirrors for reflections
or with nothing
but our knowledge of ourselves
we as a people everywhere
are for the most part
            good and kind.

A glass then if you please
held higher than the rest
to ourselves and what we each
inside our secret head aspire to be.

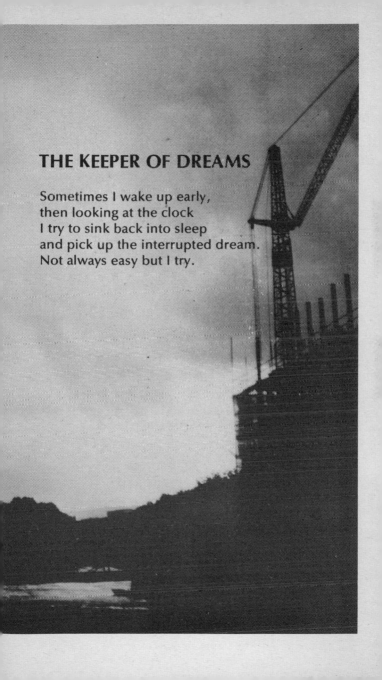

THE KEEPER OF DREAMS

Sometimes I wake up early,
then looking at the clock
I try to sink back into sleep
and pick up the interrupted dream.
Not always easy but I try.

Dreams are tickets
through the longest night.

If I could
I'd steal from time
every summer that we ran through
every Sunday we slept in
each May morning we imagined
God has made for our eyes only.

Then I'd divide them all by two
keeping half, and giving half to you.

If I had my half of all those summers
                    to thumb through
maybe the keeper of dreams
            would help me dream up
all the other seasons.

The keeper of dreams.
    The lender of hope.
Wherever he is,
he'd better come here soon
to hold me every bit as hard
as he's held back the dream.

FULL MOON

The full moon, buzz saw-like
begins to slice through lower clouds
so steadily and purposeful
it seems like only minutes
till it will roll a bit, pitch, nuzzle in
and find an eye-level niche to rest awhile.

You dare not look away
unless you're willing to turn back
and find it climbing out of sight
or overhead, beginning its descent
back down the outside of another sky.

Full moons,
like full bellies,
full-up hearts and heads
should be savored, realized
and thought about when happening.

It does no good
to try and conjure them
afterward or later in the week.
They should be noticed
as they notch the sky
        or not at all.

Whistle Stops, Revisited

Life is only little stops
along the highway,
the railroad right-of-way
or our own common corridors.
Time's the only punctuation.

WHISTLE STOPS, REVISITED

And still I go out slowly.
Out of habit, more than caution.
I pause at every landing
between the sets of stairs,
Finally I reach the door
then like a pale-skinned bather
testing water at the seaside
on the first warm day
I scrutinize the night
                    most carefully.

Will the dangers of the dark
be less plentiful this time
or still outnumber
all those small rewards?

I have been impatient
                    in the past
and in all past lives
but if age has not made of me
                a man agreeable,
still I'm less demanding.

So much beauty walks
along the sidewalk
          open and inviting.
Where once it hid upstairs
beyond the halfway open curtain
or on the porch behind a fan,
it now fans out around us
like connecting lily pads
that float along the edges
          of forbidden pools.

And so it is.
We must continue looking.
Not always just to *find*,
though that is a way to force ourselves
to join the others at the curb.

　　　　　For me at least,
I think that I am more concerned
that if I lower my binoculars
or once forget to dust my telescope
　　　　　　　　I'll lose my place.

There are always others.
Some with needs immediate.
Some who wait their turn.
Some with needs far more essential
to their heads and hearts than mine.
Some who do not, will not look at me
even if I trip them with a smile
or nudge them with a grin
and some who spring
like springbok from the underbrush.

Who does not go home alone
more often than with someone
                seen and needed?

But there are those who take in love
as easily as umbrellas close.
Perhaps they have more practice
in the art of catching others' eyes
Could be their standards are relaxed
                or put off out of need.
Far from thinking ill of them
                I wish them well.

Cities and the city street
conspire to hold dark secrets.
For some of my life
I have been helped and harbored
              by that knowledge.

Not only me
but those I met or knew
or never meet but wished to know
have found a willing confidant
on certain city streets.
The canyons that surround them
have protected one and all.

But did protection
ever really worry me?
Not honestly,
except perhaps when I was growing
and stayed within the shadows
       from the bully,
until I learned that bullies
all have three dimensions too.
Even in the taking
the meanest give back something.
       A lesson maybe.

That kind of fear
has long been absent,
replaced by new rejections.

Do I now enjoy the solitude
I always fought so hard against,
or do I go on marking time?
No excuses seem appropriate.

But I have had helpers
those who were compliant
in the deed.

Shoo! Be gone! I wish to tell them
for I am making ready for a journey.
Not one, I think, but many.

I'm aware that I've been
                    hiding.
Too long to remember.
And I will not deny
I helped create
whatever outward image
                    the world
or even those
who after hiking through the
                    subterfuge
and finding me, still have.

But I never meant it
                    not really
what I wanted most
and still go seeking
        is accessibility.

The same accessibility
I hope those coming
through my life and near to me
will find I have
          or try to have.

I cannot live up to an image
          but then who can?
Even *Image Makers*
sometimes slip on their own turf.
I've gone skating sometimes
on ice so thin
I thought the next glide
                    up ahead
would pull me down
and spirit me away.

But I nearly always
got back home to safety
some way, always, just in time.
Like Buck Rogers in the serials
or both the Hardy Boys
I made it to security.

The perils soon forgotten.
The breaks and bruises
          on the inside,
some too long in healing
will with some new feat
                    accomplished
some new derring-do well done
finally heal themselves—
or so I keep pretending
even when each new experience
seems like a millstone, not a milestone.

The walls I scaled
for whatever reason
I leapt up to like a cat.
Only once
did I jump down hard enough
to break both legs.

Guidewires high and thin
were always mine to walk along
without provision or a net,
I rode the ridges
wise enough to be a westerner.

When caught pretending anything
the lie of pleading *learning*,
was never disbelieved.

In truth
I *am* a learner
though I seldom read instructions,
I write the check to pay the fee
and pocket the permit.
I'd rather hit apprenticeship head on.

Only by working can we work
only by practice is life lived.
Only by loving do we become
                 fit to love.

I confess.
I should have gone out more.
I should have crossed the street
and left the block more often:
had I done so
    I'd have less to wish for
I'd know more
of what there is to know.

If I'd traveled
without Sunday to Sunday
             work to work
I'd not ever have the need
For some one, something new.

I would have found—
if I had taken time to do so
some body in all the somebodies
that I could have given
this locked-in, often useless thing
that I pass off as life.
Given and corrected,
straightened up and straightened out.

Because it was not made for me,
          but for someone,
it often doesn't fit.
I stretch it too far sometimes,
and there are times
I fail to give it room enough
              to grow
as lives will grow when left alone.

All that could have been
      corrected and set right
If I'd gone traveling
and wrote more notes
instead of taking cards
            and address slips
that never quite survive the laundry.

What did I learn
when I *did* go traveling?
That I could die an easy death
or live a life most bountiful
if I could lie forever motionless
within some known or unknown arms
that wrap me up within the kindly night
and leave me for the morning's mischief.

I am only one more man
trying diligently
and with as little desperation as possible
to make it safely through
            but one more day.

Life is not unlike a whistle-stop.
Better hurry. Catch the train,
                or leave it.
And within each life
are dozens more
of little pauses,
breath catchers,
time takers,
tin woes,
death.

Now I Have the Time

What day is it, you said
the next day, I replied
Oh, and you were gone.

NOW I HAVE THE TIME
(Another Monday,
Two Months Later)

Now I have the time
to take you riding
        in the car
to lie with you
in private deserts
or eat with you
in public restaurants.

Now I have the time
for football all fall long
and to apologize
for little lies and big lies
told when there was no time
to explain the truth.

I am finished
with whatever tasks
kept me from walking
in the woods with you
                    or leaping
in the Zanford sand.

I have so much time
that I can build for you
sand castles out of mortar.

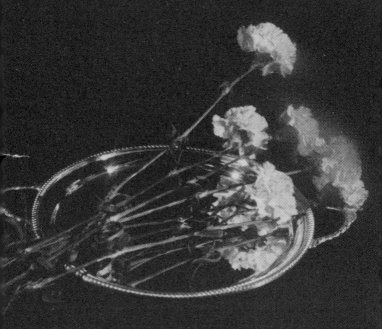

Midweek picnics.
Minding my temper in traffic.
Washing your back
and cleaning out my closets.
Staying in bed with you
long past the rush hour
and the pangs of hunger
and listening to the story
                of your life
in deadly detail.
Whatever time it takes,
I have that time.

I'd hoped that I might
take you traveling
down the block
or to wherever.

I've always wanted
to watch flowers open
all the way,
however long
the process took.

Now I have the time
to be bored
to be delivered
to be patient
to be understanding,
to give you
all the time you need.

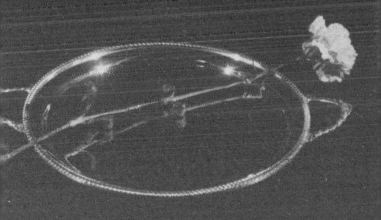

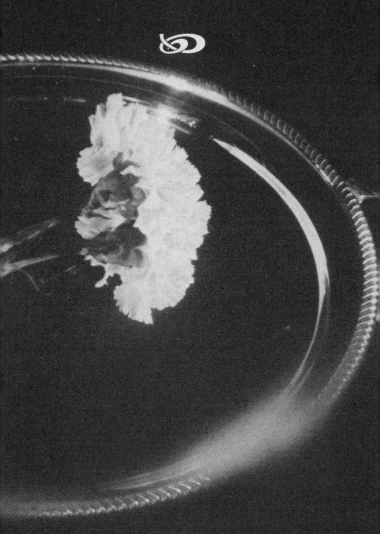

Now I have the time.
Where are you?

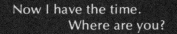

LAUGHTER
THROUGH THE CRYSTAL

Not so much for safety as for peace
do I retreat into imagination.
Retreat might be the wrong word
my mind's people take me forward.

Still imagination's devices
               do the needed job
when you're not here,
when no one's here.

Just now I've been awakened
by the screeching of mad bluejays.
The coffee isn't ready
the morning paper
won't arrive
for one more hour
No need to even think.

The Morse code of coffee perking
                            in this room
now occupied by only me says it all
like laughter through the crystal.

STAINED GLASS/MIDDLE MAY

Such patience
and such simple understanding
is so new to me
that I'm in awe
          of my control.

And yet if this
is not Land's End
then I do not expect
a better or more beautiful
                    horizon.

Our lives
will be lived out
in stained-glass glory
and new winding roads.

You teach me how
to cut and then assemble
stained and unstained glass
I'll show you all the winding roads
                I know—
and some we'll come upon together.

ROUNDABOUT

Every day
we live life to the fullest
we die a little—
          but who complains?
Not the man who props his pocket open
to catch an extra share
of unexpected rain.
Not the woman, love exhausted,
told by her lover
that she has never been more beautiful
than those few minutes
lying there half smiling
like the softest breeze
that rattles gentle leaves
at the tops of all the tallest trees.
Not the child who after school
was knocked half-winded to the ground
by a fly ball in a favorite game.

Every day we live life
hold on to it as much as the living can
we die a little more inside and out
but it's a small price to be paid
in the game of life called roundabout.

INITIAL VOYAGE

No one's moved the road for me
and no one's found a way
to beat the brush down
     through the woods
or make the brambles
snap back safely and on cue.

No clearing in the woods
awaits my coming,
foot or horseback,
except the clearing
that I make myself.

But the path to you
was never easy
and the road
that led me this far
	had no lamps
to light it.

So credit me with being
Chris Columbus for ten years
and never giving up till now.

Where once I hailed the masts
that bobbed above horizons
as my sailor kin
I picture them as rafts
in readiness just now,
not even knowing why.

Later ask the first mate
                of the Nina,
or the Pinta's engineer
they'll tell you how I smiled
even as I walked the plank.

And when I rolled upon the waves,
seaweed still between my ears,
ask them if I frowned
even when the friendly sharks
were chewing on what brains I had
before I started loving you.
They'll tell you no.
They'll tell you that I let the sea
envelop me as I enveloped you.

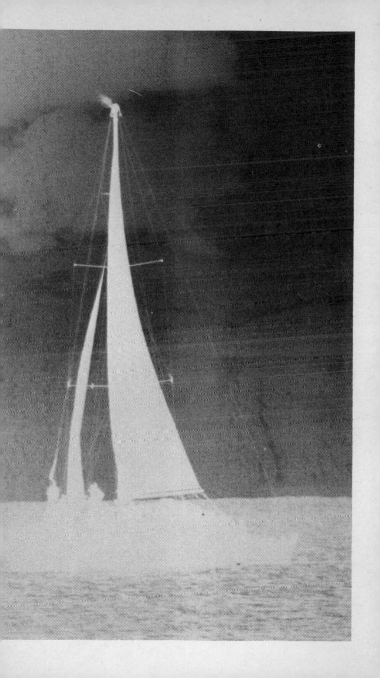

Carols of an Evening

Listen! There are bells,
    soft voices
and carols of an evening.

STANYAN STREET
1.

You lie bent up in embryo sleep
below the painting of the blue fisherman
                              without a pillow.
The checkered cover kicked
                    and tangled on the floor
the old house creaking now
a car going by
the wind
a fire engine up the hill.

I've disentangled myself from you
                    moved silently,
groping in the dark for cigarettes,
and now three cigarettes later
                         still elated
                              still afraid
I sit across the room watching you—

STANYAN

the light from the street lamp
coming through the shutters
hysterical patterns flash on the wall
sometimes when a car goes by
otherwise there is no change.
Not in the way you lie curled up.
Not in the sounds that never come from you.
Not in the discontent I feel.

You've filled completely
this first November day
with Sausalito and sign language
                    canoe and coffee
ice cream and your wide eyes.
And now unable to sleep
because the day is finally going home
because your sleep has locked me out
I watch you and wonder at you.

STANYAN

I know your face by touch when it's dark
I know the profile of your sleeping face
the sound of you sleeping.

Sometimes I think you were all sound
kicking free of covers
and adjusting shutters
moving about in the bathroom
taking twenty minutes of our precious time.

I know the hills
    and gullies of your body
        the curves
           the turns.

I have total recall of you
and Stanyan Street
because I know it will be important later.

It's quiet now.
Only the clock
moving toward rejection tomorrow
breaks the stillness.

TWO

I went back to look for you.
Not understanding the language of hello
I thought I'd speak it just the same.
I bathed.
left the window open
    and one light on.
The heat was off
and as we warmed each other
You made up
for all those dark indifferent backs
that turned from me these many months.

The room sat waiting
premeditated as a concierge's smile.

110

In the lobby
there were some roses on a table
I looked at them so long
I thought the buds had drained
the color from my face.
Finally I went up the stairs
to bed alone.

MORE WINE

Drunk I love you
sane or sober
until the wine of wanting
passes from the vintage
            to the dregs.

And as the carpenters
and the village vintner's son
make up the casks again
aiming for some year ahead,
we fill ourselves
with one another—
vintage wine.
Enough.

PHASE ONE

I wish you heady harvests
not once but four times
                every year
and earth enough
when you're in cities
to make the valleys
        of New England
and all the greenest hills
                in France
stay forever green
inside your heart.

113

PHASE TWO

The vessel's changing course.
Where it's bound for
                     I'm not sure
but it will go on
plowing through the sea
till every sea's been sailed.

Call me. Write me.
Send a message in a bottle.
I'll be within the next port
                         waiting
always in the harbor.

PHASE THREE

I think I'm managing
the turn quite well
I'm almost sure of it
I even find myself
greedy for the coming day.

Night Secrets

Secrets flow like gossip in the night.
And in the end
they remain just as unimportant.

MIRRORS

The side show
has as many sides
as men of midnight
and it shows them all
as finally we learn
all freaks are friendly
for in each of them
we see each other's faces.

The merry-go-round
goes on turning
and every face seems
        just the same
except the smiles on children
fading when their quarters end
disappearing in the rain.

WILL

I want love
for those I love
to come from all sides
not just selfish me.

If the moon can rise for me
it ought to rise for those
who comfort me, direct or indirectly,
banked by paths that take the dreamer home
even when the dreamer doesn't know
that I have willed his pleasant journey.

TEN BY TEN

In ten years
of watching you
and never knowing
that I'd share
your Christmas bed,
I'd learned to live
with just the want.

Now with no point
of reference
but your arms,
I can't go back.

SEARCH PARTY

Who is listening
under these calm stars
on this tranquil evening,
who can hear me
and who can know the sounds
my ears are hearing?

We search
because we have to search
because there is no other way.

Because the sky is low
and the world is measured
        in a child's eye
systematically we search
not places or countries
but one another's smiles
                and eyes.
There is no other way
to find ourselves
but in each other's faces

Who is listening
        here and now?
None but the lonely
I would think
for only they
would understand.
Should they lack
        understanding
they'd be the first
to care enough
about themselves
        to learn.

The lonely
are the singers
the ones who have
the loudest voices
when they finally
open up.

Sing to me
and maybe the music
from your blue guitar
will be the soothing voice
I've wished and waited for.

I have come a long way
wandering down from
silver-red mountains
in search of music
            such as yours,
so sing
and let the music
            once played
satisfy the need I have
to be among the loved
and needed people.

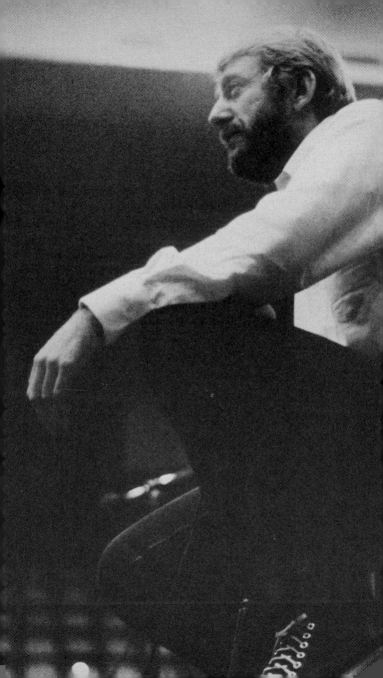

WHO KILLS THE DREAM?

Who kills the dream
and drives it into waking?
Not the owl who calls to fellow owl
predictably at one o'clock.
Not oversleep that drives me
wide awake and wall-eyed
through the center
of a drowsy,
       dreamless
not altogether hopeless night

Not the chosen memory
forgotten in convenience
or pushed aside by now.
Not tomorrow
        nor this present day
that works so hard
it earns its own
tomorrow and today.

And you are not to blame.
The you I know or will know.
The you I knew
       and don't remember.
Who then and why?
The question on the bed at borning
          and at death.
Who kills the dream and why?

Above the City

I am as locked away
in New York City
as in favored rooms
in California.

BERKELEY

The anemones wilting on the mantlepiece
the bitter brigade of umbrellas
marching past the window
queuing down the corner for the bus
and me without a sleeping pill
             waiting for what?
The rain to stop?
Inspiration to begin?
London to be kind to me?

I do not think Godot will come tonight.
But all the same I leave the window open.

ELDON, THREE

Twenty-nine flights up
the wind surrounding us
whistling, pounding
sounding like no wind
       ever sounded.

Safely
we rode out the night
       together.
When the sunlight came
you hid us both
  behind a pillow.

That first night behind us
a week now gone
a new one coming
you hide me still.
I am safe and sleepy
smiling, unafraid
ready to go forward
not walking, running
through all the storms
and all the sunshine
　　　　up ahead.

PIECES OF GLASS

Can the living
reach the dead?
Yes, I said,
as I lay dying.
And if they can't,
I heard
the unknown say,
it's not from
any lack of trying.

BOXER

I am so amazed
at finding out
my head still reels
under even friendly blows
that I'm determined
not to let the boxer
        or the battler
come in close again.

I will not willingly go out
into the evening any more
and place myself within
that enchanted circle,
the moving staircase
        or the rain.

I should stay at home
behind the iron gates
      and rainbow glass.
Sure places I've constructed.
The disappointments yet to come
can be lived by me in private.
No one need know
if the wounds are fatal
or if I'm waiting out
             some healing time.

There is an emptiness
and it is deep.
A wound so old
that healing wouldn't work.

If I have not yet
come back around
to where I started
then I am only inches
from that now narrow
                    corridor
meant to bring me there.

TEARING DOWN WALLS

No wall can stop
the coming of love
no clock can bring it back,
yet letters are still sent
on missions armies couldn't win
       for love or country.

Night Music

Not only chants
fill up the evening,
      thunder too,
but it is all night music.

THE DANCE

The strong young bulls
don't come to the ring
　　　to die on Sunday.
They come to show a man
their energy, their pride.
The dancing they have been
rehearsing all their lives
to bring to the arena
a certain afternoon in August,
for one performance only.

Their partners
are not killers then.
They're dancers too.
Their red capes flashing.
Three-cornered hats
that scoop applause
when the dancing's done.

TORO

I wrote those words
about the bullring
           long ago,
I never quite believed them then
and I don't believe them now.

I'm of the Taurus sign
and every dead bull in the ring
           is my relation.

More than that
because each creature
drawing breath within this world
was conjured by the living God,
each tail and set of ears
belongs to me as much as to
                   the matador
and I am complicit
a conspirator in his dreadful act.

BRAHMS

The clock was running down
and I had taken no precaution
for the coming night.
All the while
your arms were disengaging,
your smile receding
and your touch
not tender and not there.

Then—
      (Please don't ask me
       what the hour was)
it must have been
within the Brahms
you went to sleep unsmiling.

If I knew
then I'd forgotten
that we were loving
at your option
entangling at your convenience
and elevating one the other
only just by your design.

Unprepared I was and am
                    when any door
I thought I helped to open
                              closes.
Especially while I look the other way.

THE WALTZ

It's like a dance.
A demented waltz,
with all the dancers
just a little mad.
Loving, I mean.
Giving in, letting go.
It's like a crazy waltz.
Couples in the dance.
Close, apart, together, turning,
promising more than they can give.

A game of musical chairs.
You play to win
but why play so hard?
It's only a waltz.

I HAVE LOVED CHOPIN

I have loved Chopin
from the noon till evening.
Often when I'm leaving
a face that didn't smile
the way I'd hoped it would
makes my shoulder sag.
I turn to go
and think I hear a laugh
trailing in my wake.

I leave amid the laughter
far luckier than some
for I have loved Chopin.

Music in the distance
a dark indifferent hand
and I have loved Chopin.

I have loved Chopin
even after midnight.
Even after being held at bay
by a cold and cloudless day
I can still remember who I am
you'd know me if you saw me,
hatless in a hurry,
looking into windows
that don't look back at me
I never ever worry
for I have loved Chopin.

Music in the distance
a dark indifferent hand
and I have loved the noon tide,
I have loved the park.
I have cared for those
who wouldn't, couldn't care,
smiled at some—who,
puzzled at me, frowned.

Read the writing
and the paste-ups left to read
on a thousand walls.
Roared at lions, roaring back
and hearing music
through the walls,
I have loved Chopin.

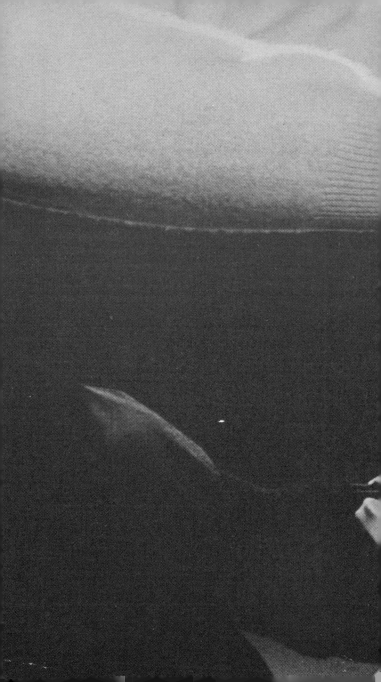

Many an Afternoon

Conscience
is a fragile thread
whistle and it flies.

PICTURE POSTCARD

She stands beneath a tree
                    that blossoms,
apple blossoms, I suppose
A smile, that on first viewing
doesn't seem correct—
but then you look again
an inner smile is somewhere there
a laugh half opening, then gone.
So thin and shy she seems,
stopped still
within a world
that she invented.

But she only waits
            to lead you in,
that is if you dare or care
            or want to come—
And who would not come running,
sneaking past the gate
and down into this orchard
she's made richer
by her dallying this day?

If I am passing by
or find some good excuse
        to do so
I never miss the chance
to pause or stop within
the doorway leading to
            Meg's office,
just to reassure myself
that it's still there.
It always is.

A picture postcard
of the shy Edna Millay
              reaching up,
or is it my imagination still,
to touch an overhanging bough
of plum or apple blossoms.

No drenched and dripping apple tree
not in this tinted photograph
only the bough that sunshine
bursts from bud to blossom.

The figure of a girl
slight and of no certain age
standing still before the camera
            of a friend
and not some lover, I suppose.
For had it been a lover
who cocked and clicked the shutter shut
the smile that was imprisoned
down these years
        for me to see
would have been much wider.

My appreciation
of the camera's blink
has never been so strong,
nor have I marveled more—
even standing in an orchard
          my own self—
at the beauty of a tree
So filled with blossoms
it might lean and fall.

Meg bent over piles of words
that crowd her desk
       like double anthills
and on the bookcase just in sight
            a picture postcard.

Now softly in the whisper
             of a whisper
You can almost hear
the girl inside the postcard say,
I will be the gladdest thing
             under the sun!
I will touch a hundred flowers
             and not pick one.

BROWNSTONE

Birds and butterflies
dart
     down
            canyons
between tall buildings
looking for a place to hide
as the sky above the city darkens
and the rain begins
          timid at first—unsure
then creeping onto window ledges
and foraging along the sidewalk.

They're tearing down
the building across the street
and the old woman
who sat cushion high
behind the flower boxes
                    is gone.
Even the children
who played along the broken sidewalk
                    have disappeared
and their hopscotch lines are washed away.

Only the multicolored cat
preening in the shop window
is unconcerned as night begins.

SEVENTY-SEVENTH STREET, 1977

Women in doorways
breasts heaving heavy
slow—sometimes not at all.
The first long day of spring
has beat, confused them all.

Newspaper fans
spread out and twittering
say whatever must be said,
the women make no words.

Bare-bellied men
staring out, hanging out
of second-story windows
scratch themselves,
pat their stomachs.

Will the weather break?
Everyone says *no*,
even subway trains
coming from the ground,
           now overhead
              agree.

Babies go on
crying in their cradles,
kids on play-streets
open fire hydrants
and soak themselves.
Adults look on in envy.

*Ready or not
here I come.*

176

Four hundred thousand
grandmas rock away
on as many porches.

Now the men are back again
at windowsills
beer cans in each hand.
When autumn comes
                for sure
I'll join a gym.

Today I'd like to know
the face of someone, anyone
I could blame my headache on.

THE TENDER EARTH

You wonder why I like the ground.
Why I like to run along the sand
and take my lovers down to riverbanks
to say the kind of things
that one should say in little rooms.

The ground is all the home I've ever had.
The only thing that I can trust
and having come up from the earth
I think sometimes I'll not get back
                              soon enough.

If I had to love something
more than the night,
more than tomorrow,
more than the sea and yesterday,
I'd choose the earth.

We'll sit a while, talk, listen,
learn each other's worth,
and come together silently
against the tender earth.

LIGHTHOUSE

Because imagination sticks
gets caught
settles in as we grow older
finally there is only
one long, silent hour
even if it lasts a day.

Have we been living
all our years for this?
It may be so.
It well may be
the size of life
is measured by the hours,
years and days it takes
for each of us to turn
within the circle
of the slowest dance.

Where then and why
how does the eagle
or the falcon fly?
And if the rabbit runs
does he run forward
            or run back?

The eagle
and the falcon too
are foragers,
but self-propelled.

Lucky rabbit
always running to his lair
and always, always
finding something there.

I think perhaps
that we are running, yes.
Always away and not toward.

I think that we are looking
not quite for the end
but for a slow dance done
upon the killing ground.

The damage we inflict
in love or hate
or any other name it's given
is usually beyond repair.

Noticed and attended to
                too late.

Too late, too late,
the maiden cried . . .
in every gothic ever read
and it's the same
face down in goose down pillows
or crying uselessly
        in unmade beds.

What then can we give
or promise one the other?
Ourselves? We try,
but always we hold back.
More promises?

So few are kept
that credibility
must now be stitched
or sewn together.

Finally, the answer
comes up once again,
we can offer one another
nothing but the rattle
of destructive words
a slow death
on the killing ground.
So much for love
    and mornings.

THE MUD KIDS

Out of the curious foraging rain
moving over the lawn like evening,
one by one they come,
               the mud kids.
Carrying their mud in buckets,
sometimes hardened into bricks
or molded into Ken & Barbie dolls.
The ones who claim
we never understand them.

The truth is
I don't think we do
anymore than we allow ourselves
the proximity and love
of these our children
that might enable them
                    to know us.

We blame it all on Freud.
A Madison Avenue cult of youth.
The decline of moral standards.
Urban nonrenewal.
Dylan songs that taught them
a rudimentary privilege
most of them had yet to learn
                    at home,
the process of thought.

We call this failure
        to communicate
anything but what it is,
the turning from homes
that weren't quite right
and getting up from TV dinners
to eat the snow,
the playing with each other
instead of dolls.

Let the mud kids make their pies
and throw them at the world.
With their help
it might turn out to be
a better place to live in.

And, anyway,
Mack Sennett would be proud.

After Midnight Passes

Consider
the in-between:
Midnight gone,
dawn still sleeping.
You the only one awake.

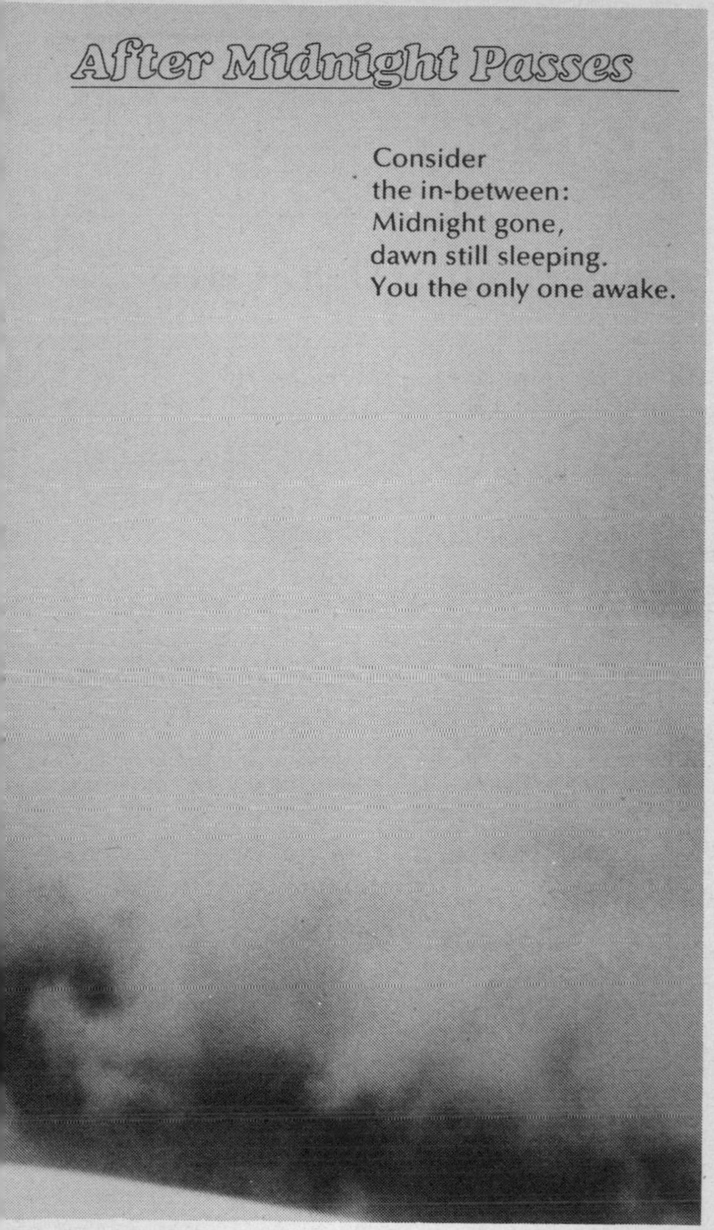

PHANTOM SLEIGH BELLS

There you are and there you go
you didn't and you couldn't
and now you'll never know
you only helped the sadness
speed a little faster
down the road toward me.
But, I've learned to live
with demons you and no one else
could ever know.

In a way, it helps
that you don't understand
let me look upon you
as the mover of some mountains
I could never move
that way I can be the kind of man
I always hoped to be.

EARTHQUAKE

Sometimes we want so much
we never stop to think
men are that way, you know.
They have a special need
a need so great
it pushes back all reasoning.

I could have said that I was sorry.
That would have been a lie.
It would have been untrue
                    to feel ashamed
to feel that what we did was wrong.

You were smiling afterward
and so there must have been
some goodness there for you as well.
An earthquake? No.
A tremor, maybe.
But there are earthquakes
in your arms to come.

TREMOR

A sound now—
down the street.
       The church.
An anthem or a requiem.
The smile of God maybe
       saying, o.k.
          okay.

The legs.
The rounded buttocks.
The oval ending thighs,
all mine—all mine.
The breasts—loose now,
                    heavy now,
mine.

THE OLD HOTEL

The old hotel
sits back a block
beyond the boardwalk.
Grey in color,
     once green
     once yellow
and once maroon in trim
if chipped paint tells the truth.

There is no walk
and if there was a walk before
surely it was made of pilings
like those that now pretend to make
a stairway leading to a piling porch.

Inside,
a satin shade
balancing atop a narrow pole
is lamp and light enough
and so the lobby's dark as Sodom.

And though I haven't seen
the Nile-green horsehair sofa
sulking at the far end of the room
I know it's there
dirty as the hand of Death
sat upon and spat upon.
Drooping like a cardboard medal
on the chest of all mankind.

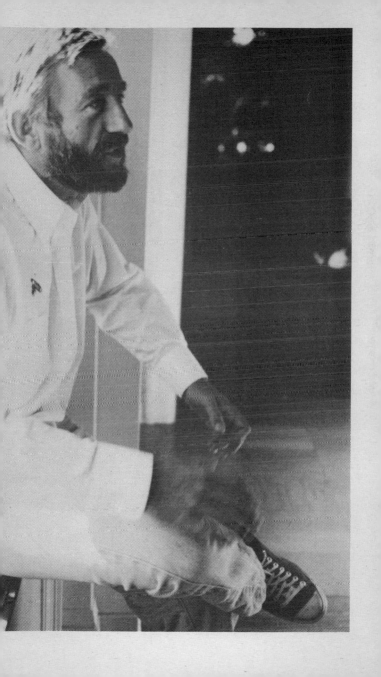

New Directions

We do not always
travel roads
of reason.

STARGAZING

I'm floating
spread-eagled
held down by stars.
I want to believe you
because I want you
and so I believe.
I do.

But what a wonder
you
close on me and caring
saying that you care.

Stay
I'm coming over there.
Better. Best.

I am floating
spread-eagled
lifted up by stars.

A FIST FULL OF SNOW

I need familiars
your bowels and brains have to be
as sure for me as both your eyes.
Passing through the sheets
and climbing down inside of you—
                    even though
you give back one for one
              and maybe more
I sometimes wonder if I haven't
traversed or gone climbing down a shaft
so new that none, not even me
        had charted it.

Did you take a turn that I missed?
        Did I go somewhere else?
Was there a curve we didn't
                go around together? Worse—
has someone else been hiking
down your highway?
Not to worry, never mind
                change is change
unaccountable but surprising
        if you like surprises.

It's just that I had hoped
                all our surprises
would be together—planned.

There is some silence now
like dead wood in the forest
moving only when it's prodded

And I stand here waiting
with a fist full of snow.

INITIATION

I am ready
white-skinned still
not yet stolen by the summer
                or by anyone.

I am ready, even eager
for the initiation.

I don't know
what I should expect—
freedom from myself?
But I have not felt bound.
A dimension added.
But what is lacking?

I've seen the shadow people
                    gathering
talking of their runs and rallies
but I have never
              gone with them,
always hanging on the fringe.

The major and the minor keys
have intrigued me, yes.
As those that dangle do
but I have been content
to move within the music
                    that I made
playing only those passages
I was sure of
on instruments that needed
                    little amplification.

What rings there were
were only rings of sound
that shattered
and then joined
      the silence.

I have been curious
but never this close.
There was no need
to know or to experiment
without instruction.

I know you won't believe me
but I have never known
what it was like
wearing the ring all day
then dealing with the swelling
                    at night.

Whatever toys I've had
were broken by myself
not meant as instruments
                    for the breaking.

I am ready
   for *your* way.

Help me
with the breakthrough
so that the initiation
      can be over.

It's very cold in here.

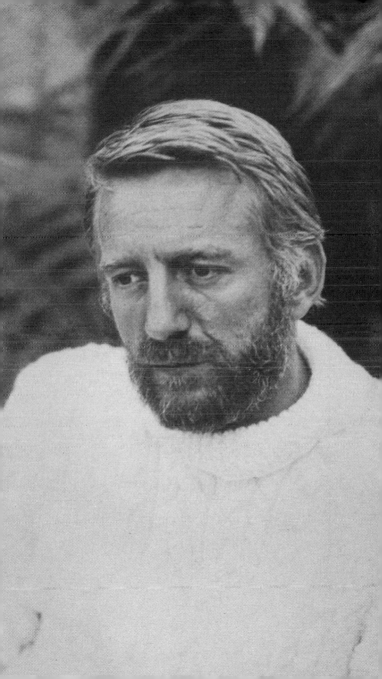

AUTUMN

Moths fill up the morning
and spiders slide down shafts
            of sunlight.

It is the autumn of the year.
The wind now makes a long,
                   slow moan.
Tired of all the old Octobers
the moan is more a sigh.
Resigned and lonely like those of us
               who face the wind
the wind itself on seeing autumn
             runs to hide.

SOME SILENT SPRING

Some silent spring
when everything is so quiet
only the piper down the field
can be heard,
we'll take the season
   at its word.
I'll bring you willows
from the woods' edge
wc'll sit still
   quietly
waiting for the deer to come
into the clearing
   for water.

Only now and then
will we look skyward
to watch the wild geese
passing in formation overhead
a dozen skybound squadrons
returning north
            going home
                beginning again
                    starting all over.
And maybe we can start again
                        ourselves.
Maybe. With the help of Spring.

MAYA

Come in she says
Why waste your evenings
                counting stars
Ah, but if I don't who will?

What astronomer
will chart the Milky Way
discovering as I do nightly
that it changes, really does
                from night to night.
Somebody has to chronicle
the stars and tides.

Space junk too.
The mist amid the stars
                    so full of it
that we can almost see
each gleaming garbage bag
jettisoned by astro-cosmonauts
traveling from west to east
                    and east to west.

Come in she says
Why waste your evenings
              counting stars?
Ah, but if I don't who will?

FROM PROMISE TO PROMISE

I sometimes wonder
why people make promises
they never intend to keep.
Not in big things
    like love or elections—
but in the things that count.

The newspaper boy
who says he'll save an extra paper
       and doesn't.
The laundry that tells you
your suit will be ready
       on Thursday
and it isn't.

Love?
Well,
        yes.
But like everything else
as we go from day to day
we move
    from promise to promise.

I've had a good many promises now
so I can wait for the harvest
and some of them to come about.

REALITY

It lies just over there.
No longer out of reach,
no longer separated
from what we thought it was.
We now know what it is
and how to call it
                    what it is.

For years
whole lifetimes, maybe
we passed it off as boredom.
It's only now we recognize it
by its real name. Peace.

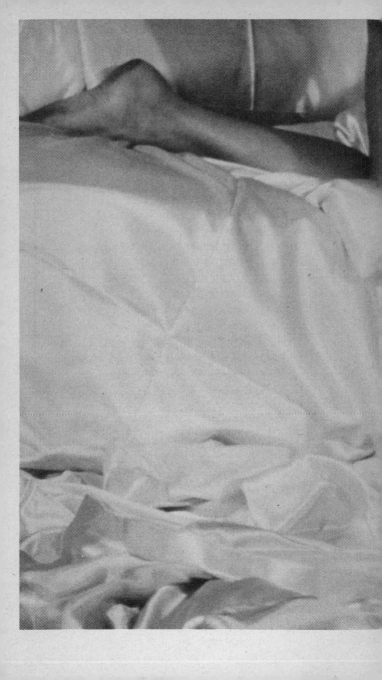

BRINGING IT FORWARD

Come, midnights one and all
come, afternoons as well
and all you early evenings.
I am ready, raring, recharged
and certainly unafraid.
If there are still too many midnights
that means for sure there are enough.

Why does it take so long
to learn life's most important lesson,
how to look at things
in more than just a single way?

Rod McKuen has traveled the world pursuing more than a dozen occupations—although he is best known as a poet, composer, columnist, lecturer and performer. As recipient of the 1978 Carl Sandburg Award, he was acclaimed "the people's poet—because he has made poetry a part of so many people's lives." With poetry that is able to touch directly the heart of the reader, it is of little wonder that McKuen's books have sold in excess of 30 million copies and that his work is taught and studied in schools, colleges, universities and seminaries throughout the world.

Among the many awards Mr. McKuen has received are the Freedom's Foundation Medal of Honor, the First Amendment Society Man of the Year Award, the University of Detroit Humanitarian Award, the Horatio Alger Award and the Man of the Year Citation from the Menninger Foundation. In addition, he was named Entertainer of the Year by the Shriners Club and has received numerous Golden Globe and Grammy awards.

With over 2,000 songs (accounting for sales of over 200 million records) to his credit, McKuen is one of the most prolific composer/lyricists writing today. His music ranges from gold-record popular standards (such as *Jean, If You Go Away, Love's Been Good to Me, Seasons in the Sun, The World I Used to Know, I'll Catch the Sun*) to widely performed classical compositions which have joined the standard repertoire of leading symphony, choral and chamber groups internationally. His suite for orchestra and narrator entitled *The City,* a commissioned work for the Louisville Orchestra, received a nomination for a Pulitzer Prize in Music. Other major McKuen classical compositions have been premiered at Carnegie Hall, London's Royal Albert Hall, the Hollywood Bowl, the Concertgebouw in Amsterdam and the Brahmsaal in Vienna.

The Black Eagle—McKuen's new "gothic musical" is of operatic scope incorporating dance, solo and ensemble choral work and filmic effects. Already a best-selling album, the show itself is scheduled to debut during the 1981-82 season with offers from Europe, Australia, Canada and the United States as possible world premiere sites prior to an international tour.

In his travels, Rod McKuen has given over 2,000 concerts and lectures in twenty-five countries over the past decade. He recently spent nearly a year in the Soviet Union writing the music and co-writing the narration for *The Unknown War*— a twenty-hour documentary feature film co-produced by Russian and American film companies. 1980 brought television specials in Europe, three tours of the U.S. and a triumphant thirty-five-performance return to Australia culminating in a documentary about Australia's new gold rush which McKuen co-produced, wrote, scored and appeared in.

The coming year will take him to China, the Middle East, throughout Europe and behind the Iron Curtain for new writing and performing projects. With the completion of three new books (*Too Many Midnights, The Rod McKuen Book of Days*, and *The Beautiful Strangers*) in 1981, the author has turned his attention to several new projects. The American Dance Ensemble for the fourth consecutive year will premiere a new major McKuen ballet work, *The Man Who Tracked the Stars*, the signs of the zodiac set to music and dance. Eight ballets previously commissioned by the company have entered its permanent repertoire and are being toured.

While not traveling, for pleasure or on tour, Rod McKuen spends most of his time in a rambling Spanish house in Southern California and in a New York apartment overlooking the Manhattan skyline.

Sources

Index to First Lines